Original title:
Thistle Thoughts

Copyright © 2025 Creative Arts Management OÜ
All rights reserved.

Author: Elias Montgomery
ISBN HARDBACK: 978-1-80566-792-6
ISBN PAPERBACK: 978-1-80566-812-1

Whispers from the Wilds

In the meadows where oddities play,
A dandelion wears its crown of gray.
Grasshoppers gossip, they chirp and hop,
While daisies wiggle, they just can't stop.

Butterflies dance with a twist and a twirl,
While a grumpy old snail gives a skeptical whirl.
The sunflowers laugh, with their heads held high,
At the clumsy ants, who can't seem to fly.

A frog in a puddle croaks out a tune,
While a squirrel in a tree sings to the moon.
All the wild things, so quirky and bright,
Join in the fun, from morning till night.

So if you wander in nature's delight,
Listen closely, you'll hear with delight.
For the wild's full of whispers, and shenanigans, too,
Where laughter and joy spring from skies of blue.

Delicate Defiance Beneath the Surface

In gardens green, they poke and prod,
With prickly kisses, they dare the odd.
A cheeky dance on a sunny day,
Laughing at woes in a spiky way.

They say, 'Oh please, do come and play!'
With every step, one must ballet.
These thorns are soft, just like a joke,
In their delightful chaos, we'll poke.

Nature's Velvet Armor

Soft as whispers, sharp they stand,
Velvet cloaks in a prickly band.
Winking at bees that make a fuss,
In this wild realm, who can we trust?

A jesting crown for bold hearts near,
With roots that giggle, full of cheer.
Nature's jesters, they don't take care,
Dressed to the nines, yet full of flair.

Grappling with the Unforgiving Bloom

Amid the green, a laughter sprouts,
With tangled weeds and silly doubts.
A vibrant fight through the afternoon,
Blooms wrestle hard, a comical tune.

With petals here and thorns of jest,
Each bloom a prank, it's all a test.
Roses and weeds in a playful clash,
Nature's laughter in a colorful flash.

A Dance with the Untamed Winds

Twisting, turning, in breezy play,
The wildflowers sway, come what may.
They laugh as the winds toss them 'round,
In this silly waltz, joy is found.

Each gust a giggle, each swirl a jest,
Nature's humor, it knows no rest.
With every tug and every pull,
Spiky dancers, hearts oh so full.

Wildly Fractured Mind

In the garden of my brain,
Ideas sprout like weeds,
Some are sharp, some are plain,
All come with quirky needs.

Juggling thoughts like juggling swords,
One slips here, another flies,
There's laughter in the discord,
And giggles where reason dies.

The shapes my thoughts create,
Can poke and prod for fun,
Like a jester on a plate,
Eating cake while on the run.

A mind that's wild, unconfined,
Dances on the edge of sanity,
Somewhere in this fray, I find,
The humor in the vanity.

Threads of a Prickled Tale

Once I threaded through a patch,
With needles made of quirk,
Each stitch a vibrant catch,
Dancing with nonchalant smirk.

The tales they tell, oh so tall,
Of pricks and playful flair,
In a bouncy, goofy sprawl,
I tumble without a care.

In the fabric of my day,
Laughter seams that intertwine,
Each prick a vibrant array,
Tingles of the grand design.

As I weave this silly yarn,
A tapestry of jest,
With every stitch, I can't discern,
If I'm foolish or just blessed.

Insights Among the Spikes

Peeking through the jagged green,
I find a spark of cheer,
Among the sharp, there's more to glean,
A chuckle smuggled near.

Each spike a curious thought,
Pointing out the fun,
The wisdom that it's wrought,
Makes light of what's begun.

In the wild where notions sting,
A comedy unfolds,
With every prick, a little zing,
As the truth quietly scolds.

So here I dance, all meek and spry,
Among the sharp and bold,
With laughter lifting me up high,
As life's stories are retold.

Braided with Shadows

In a braid of leafy cheer,
Shadows whisper jests,
Where echoes chortle near,
And folly feels its best.

Twisted paths of whimsy flow,
Entwined with laughter's light,
Each turn a punchline's glow,
A play that feels so right.

Hiding in the tangled mess,
Are giggles, soft and sweet,
Wrapped up in nonsense dress,
Dancing on my busy feet.

With shadows blending in a game,
I step out, cheerful, bold,
For every thorn, a joy to frame,
As the silly tales unfold.

The Language of Jagged Leaves

In a garden, whispers flow,
Where plants talk fast, and gossip grow.
Their jagged edges slice the air,
While the daisies laugh without a care.

A rogue bee buzzes, thinks he's wise,
But he trips and falls, oh what a surprise!
The sun's bright glare leads him astray,
Leaving him dizzy, wishing to play.

Cursed Roots and Cradled Hopes

Among the soil, secrets hide,
Roots entangled, squishy inside.
Each plant dreams of tastier treats,
But often gets stuck in sticky feats.

A worm complains of backaches tight,
While the seedlings laugh with sheer delight.
Hopes cradled in dirt, so very deep,
They giggle at shadows, wake from their sleep.

Wild Thoughts in a Prickly Existence

A hedgehog thinks he's quite the star,
When rolling around, he wanders far.
But prickly thoughts bring prickly ends,
And even the breeze seems to make amends.

Silly squirrels chuckle in trees,
As they watch him tumble with such ease.
With every roll, a laugh bestowed,
In this wild life on a bumpy road.

Sunlight Amidst the Spines

Sunshine bursts through sharpest crowns,
Creating laughter, despite the frowns.
Prickles glimmer, a sparkling show,
As the garden sways to the rhythm of glow.

A ladybug flits, so boldly bright,
Dancing on edges, a comical sight.
With each little jig, she breaks the norm,
In a world of chaos, she's the calm before storm.

Navigating the Wild Thorns

In a garden lush, I do roam,
Finding my way, far from home.
Dodging sharp quills, I just might slip,
On a rogue branch, I lose my grip.

A bee buzzes by, playing the fool,
While I try to look oh-so-cool.
I dance in circles, arms in the air,
A sight so bizarre, folks stop and stare.

Each prickly poke, a little tease,
Hoping to find my inner peace.
But laughter erupts, the thorns just cheer,
As I envision myself as a deer.

With a hop and a skip, I dash away,
From green little fiends that wish to play.
In this wild patch, where chaos springs,
There's joy in the jabs that mischief brings.

A Tangle of Emotions

Lost in a jumble, my head's in a spin,
A heartfelt maze where do I begin?
With a giggle and wiggle, I tumble along,
Making up stories, where all can belong.

Caught in a web, of laughter and jest,
Who needs a map? I'll just be a guest.
Trying to untangle each knot and twist,
Finding the fun in a moment missed.

A laugh with a sigh, emotions collide,
With prickly sentiments I can't abide.
I wear my heart like a colorful hat,
A silly parade, just imagine that!

As laughter flickers like stars on the lake,
From chaos and thorns, my own path I make.
Embracing the wild, where fun surely swells,
My tangled heart sings, in joyous spells.

Resilience in Bloom

In the face of pricks, I raise a cheer,
For every scratch tells tales, my dear.
With petals bright and whispers of glee,
I'll turn these thorns into a jubilee.

I wobble and giggle at brambles I meet,
Finding a bounce in my once weary feet.
Each little poke, a hilarious trek,
Making mischief, what the heck!

With roots that burrow deep in the ground,
A sprout of courage where joy is found.
Amid the thicket, I dance and zoom,
Flamboyant, I bloom, defying the gloom.

So raise your glass to this wild fight,
For resilience can shine in the chaos of night.
With laughter and blooms, let's take a look,
At the bright side of life, come on, let's cook!

Shadows at Midnight

As moonlight casts a playful spell,
Beneath the thorns, I grin and dwell.
Shadows dance, the night's a hoot,
With prickers on guard, in festive pursuit.

A giggle escapes amid the dark cool,
While I mock the thorns, so sharp and cruel.
As mischief ensues, the sprites join in,
Tickling my sides with their raucous din.

Every sad moment, like a fleeting breeze,
Is met by a laugh, if you just tease.
For shadows might threaten us, that is their game,
But joy in the thicket will never be tamed.

With raucous laughter that tickles the night,
I'll waltz through the thorns, my heart full of light.
So here's a toast to the midnight spree,
Where shadows bring giggles, wild and free.

Woven into the Weeds

In a garden lush with dreams,
The weeds dance like silly teams.
They giggle and twist, all so spry,
While the daisies watch with a sigh.

A gopher takes a sneak peek,
With a grin that's far from meek.
He chases the butterflies around,
While the sage just stands its ground.

The roses blush in bright delight,
As the grasshoppers jump with might.
A bee buzzes a tune so sweet,
While the garden throws a wild beat.

A Thicket of Ideas

In a thicket where thoughts collide,
Wacky ideas take off for a ride.
One thought wears a polka-dot hat,
While another tries to dance with a cat.

Silly voices echo the trees,
As squirrels imitate the buzzing bees.
With notions both crazy and grand,
They plot adventures through dreamland.

A pondering mushroom joins the fray,
Saying nonsense and leading astray.
The breeze carries laughter on its way,
Tickling each leaf in wild ballet.

Prickly Dreams

In a field where prickers play,
Dreams keep poking the sun's rays.
A dandelion sneezes, oh dear!
And the clouds giggle, full of cheer.

Prickly ideas sprout from the ground,
With a quirky sense of humor found.
They weave wild stories, sharp and sly,
As the crickets join in, oh my!

The stars wink back from their high perch,
While the cactus does a little lurch.
With each prick a tale comes alive,
In the madness where laughter thrives.

The Enigma of Flora

Amidst the blooms, a riddle grows,
Flora whispers secrets, who knows?
A daffodil hums a tune so bright,
Trying to wink in the soft moonlight.

The violets gossip, saying things,
While the tulips flaunt their colorful flings.
A butterfly twirls, a curious sight,
As petals chuckle with pure delight.

The mystery deepens, shadows play,
In laughter's garden, a wild display.
With a wink from a fern and a cheeky smirk,
Flora's enigma is a whimsical perk.

Blooms Beneath the Hard Edge

Beneath a prickly crown, they dance,
In hidden patches, they take a chance.
With smiles they sprout, and laughter grows,
In places where nobody else knows.

A jester's cap of purple hue,
They poke and prod with humor true.
With every twist, a giggle feeds,
These rebel blooms, they plant their seeds.

The Complexities of Green

Oh, the shades of green that tease the eyes,
Some are shy, while others rise.
A kaleidoscope of moods and quirks,
In the garden where the mischief lurks.

Emerald jokes and jade surprise,
They twinkle bright and catch the skies.
Nature's canvas, a jester's booth,
Where every leaf holds a bit of truth.

Surrendering to the Spines

In a world of spines, it's wise to laugh,
For pokey friends give a jolly half.
They poke fun but never stay,
A scrappy lot who like to play.

Embrace the prickles, dance in delight,
For where there's laughter, fears take flight.
In every jab, a jest is born,
Through laughter's lens, we'll not be torn.

Twisting Pathways of Thought

Paths that twist like giggling vines,
Each turn reveals new punchline signs.
A mental maze with snickers inside,
Where wild ideas take a joyride.

In this labyrinth of whimsy and zest,
Every dark corner holds a jest.
With foliage thoughts that leap and bound,
In every crease, a chuckle is found.

The Thorned Mind

In a garden where ideas bloom,
A prickly thought may find some room.
It dances round like a cheeky sprite,
With laughter that escapes at night.

Tik-tok goes the brain's wild game,
Where wild ideas never feel the shame.
A thorny joke finds its way to light,
Leaving us giggling at its silly bites.

Witty banter grows like weeds,
Among the thorns, it plants its seeds.
In the chaos, we find the fun,
Chasing thoughts 'til the day is done.

A jester's mind can dance and weave,
Crafting stories we can believe.
With thorns like armor, we will show,
How laughter makes the spirit glow.

Beneath the Surface of Spines

Underneath the pointy guise,
Lies a world of goofy sighs.
Where spiky thoughts come out to play,
In a quirky, upside-down ballet.

Each spine a twist, a jest concealed,\nA riddle wrapped in a leafy shield.
We poke and prod, we laugh and tease,
Finding humor in all the unease.

When did we think that pain was wise?
With every jab, we find a prize.
Inside the prickles, there's delight,
Like hidden treasures in the night.

So let's explore this garden wild,
Where even thorns can be beguiled.
Beneath each edge, a chuckle waits,
Just peek inside, and laugh with mates.

Echoes from the Bramble

In the bramble, whispers spin,
Funny tales where all begins.
A rustling leaf, a giggling sound,
In nature's jokes, hilarity found.

Echoes bounce from pointy peaks,
They tickle our minds and tease our cheeks.
With every rustle, we share a grin,
Brambling laughter, let the fun begin.

Now take a stroll through paths not straight,
Where humor grows, we congregate.
In every corner, a giggle sprouts,
Even the flowers wonder about.

So if you hear a chuckle near,
Don't be surprised; it might be clear.
The bramble holds the best of memes,
In a world of laughter, we chase our dreams.

Soft Resilience

Beneath the guise of prickly wear,
Lies a softness that's beyond compare.
With every laugh, we find our grace,
Even thorns can have a friendly face.

Resilient hearts will dance and sway,
Through clumsy steps, we find our way.
A poke here, a jab there,
Yet in the laughter, we find repair.

Life's a jest, a playful tease,
Where little bumps turn into ease.
So bring your smile and let it shine,
For soft resilience is divine.

Through every thorn, we'll venture forth,
Discovering joy in what it's worth.
With laughter on this thorny ride,
A merry heart, our faithful guide.

The Sharp Edge of Memory

I stumbled on a memory sharp,
Like a cactus in the park.
A laugh that burst like morning sun,
But left a tiny little mark.

I danced through days of yesteryear,
In socks that didn't quite fit right.
Each step a giggle, every slip,
A tumble into pure delight.

I recall a time with popsicle sticks,
Building dreams that often fell.
But the taste of sweetness lingered on,
I'd craft my stories, oh so well.

Yet now I trip on playful dreams,
And giggle at the past with glee.
With edges soft, and laughs so bright,
Those prickly memories set me free.

Thorns of Reflection

In mirrors made of shattered glass,
I find a face that wears a grin.
A poke from thoughts that sharp as thorns,
Yet each prick brings a little win.

I ponder jokes on life's cruel stage,
Where laughter bloomed in awkward ways.
With every thorn, a lesson learned,
I'll laugh at life's peculiar plays.

Reflecting on my tangled trails,
Where every misstep tickled pink.
The thorns remind with gentle jabs,
That humor helps us not to sink.

So here's to all the prickly paths,
To every twist that made me smile.
I'll wear my thorns like badges bright,
And dance through life, just for a while.

Petal and Spine

A flower stood with confidence,
Decked out in polka-dot attire.
Its petals bright in sunny hues,
But oh! The spine was quite a liar.

With every swing, it poked a friend,
While giggles echoed through the garden.
A game of chase with nature's quirks,
The laughs turned into pure pardon.

The petals fluffed and twisted round,
A jester dancing with a grin.
Yet hidden sharpness paid no mind,
To all the joy that bloomed within.

So let us cheer for every bloom,
Especially those with hidden charms.
For life's a riot full of fun,
Even with the sharpest arms.

Blooming in the Chaos

In messy rooms where laughter reigns,
The chaos feels like art divine.
With socks tossed high and toys askew,
Each day is a wacky design.

I can't find where my shoes have gone,
They're playing hide and seek again.
But giggles sprout from every mess,
A treasure hunt that brings no pain.

The world's a flowerbed of quirks,
Each petal seems to wear a frown.
Yet with a poke here and a laugh there,
We turn the gloom to comic crown.

So here's to all the tangled threads,
The blooms that blossom in disarray.
With happy hearts and spirits light,
We find the fun in every fray.

A Field of Conundrums

In a meadow where conundrums bloom,
Questions dance like flowers, making room.
With each riddle wrapped tight in a leaf,
Giggles sprout, defying belief.

Would you rather taste shoes or a hat?
Debates linger like a wily old cat.
Each oddity walks with a swagger and shine,
In this garden of nonsense, all twine and entwine.

What if clouds were made of whipped cream?
A sky full of sundaes, that's quite the dream!
They'd float on by, in a sugary spree,
Where each fluffy bite invites you to flee.

So roam through this field of curious jest,
Where laughter grows tall, and odd thoughts invest.
In this quirky patch, let your worries be light,
And find joy in the riddle, a delightful sight.

Secrets of the Burr

In the shadows where secrets lay tight,
A burr sits grinning, a mischievous sight.
Woven tales of stuck socks in the wash,
And socks that tango — a colorful slosh.

It cuddles up close to those who won't see,
A silent partner in chaotic glee.
"Is that a burr on your arm or a friend?"
Both might just stick till the very end.

Each twist of its nature is full of surprise,
Like a prank-happy clown with glittery eyes.
"So you thought you could escape my embrace?"
The burr just cackles and quickens the chase.

So take heed of the tales that these burrs can spin,
Like an old merry-go-round, it draws you in.
For just when you think it has let go your shoe,
It's marking the spot, "I'm still here, boo-hoo!"

Echoes of the Grit

In a place where echoes bounce off the wall,
Lives a sneaky grit that waits for a call.
It pops up like corn when you least expect,
Making mischief, the rascally elect.

"Did you hear that?" it whispers with glee,
A cheerfully annoying little NPC.
"I'm a bump in the night, a squeak in the floor,
A tickle of sand in your favorite drawer."

It winks at the moon, and dances with light,
A comical figure in shadows of night.
"Why fix what's not broken? Isn't it grand?
To trip over giggles, don't you understand?"

So listen real close to the echoes around,
For in every silly sound, joy can be found.
Like laughter repeated in a silly old play,
This grit will remind you to chuckle and stay.

The Beauty of Discomfort

In a world where comfort comes wearing a cape,
It hides all the fumbles, the slips and the scrape.
But there's beauty in awkward, a charm in the fall,
Like a penguin on ice, laughing through it all.

A shoe that's too tight? What great comedy!
A dance of the toes, a wild symphony.
Embrace the tight pants and wiggles they force,
Life's a circus, jump, and stay on your course.

At dinner, the broccoli could stage a revolt,
As dinner rolls scatter — oh, the silly jolt!
But with each little mishap, there's a spark of delight,
In a world of discomfort, laugh till it's bright.

So cherish the moments that make you unsure,
For in every cringe, there's a joy to allure.
When you trip on the punchline, just giggle and grin,
For the beauty of not knowing makes life a win!

Lost in the Green Maze

In a field so wide, I lose my way,
With greens so bright, they seem to play.
Spiky friends poke out in glee,
I'm the lost one, can't you see?

Bumblebees buzz with a silly grin,
Dancing around, oh where to begin?
I trip on roots, oh what a sight,
Nature laughs at my mid-day plight.

I follow a squirrel, so full of sass,
He stops and stares as I trip on grass.
With leaves for a crown, I strut like a king,
But where's that path? Oh, this is a sting!

Under a tree, I sit for a break,
Wondering why I had to take the shake.
Nature smirks with a side of cheer,
Who knew getting lost could bring such beer?

The Thicket of Awakening

Woke up one morn in a green surprise,
Surrounded by prickers, oh what a rise!
Thought I was dreaming, still half awake,
And here comes the worm, for goodness' sake!

The leaves are giggling, the grass, a speck,
As I try to figure out this thorny trek.
A squirrel gives me a disapproving look,
While I fumble about like a cheeky crook.

"Help me!" I yell to a passing bee,
But he just buzzes and laughs with glee.
In this thicket where sunlight is sparse,
I dance like a fool and make my heart farce.

Amidst all the prickles, a flower bids,
"Join the party, come on, don't kid!"
So I twirl and spin, my worries cast,
In this awakening, I'm free at last!

Shadows Cast by Spines

In shadows where spines boldly sway,
I tiptoe softly, come what may.
A clumsy hare hops, slips on a chard,
While I giggle here, with my foolish regard.

The whispers of grasses tease my ear,
"Be careful of scrapes, we hold our cheer!"
A cactus chuckles, "You can't poke fun,"
While I dance with shadows, oh what a run!

A parade of critters passes through,
With tiny haloes, life's colorful crew.
The sun sets low, casting mischief brown,
As I laugh and trip on my leafy gown.

Each spine a jester with armor leased,
They quip and twist, always least.
Yet here I stand, in shadows profound,
With laughter and prickers, joy's always found!

Gazing at the Gold

In a sea of green, I spot some gold,
A glimmering dream, worth more than told.
I rush like a kid to grab the prize,
Until a nettle gives me a surprise!

The petals wave like a royal flag,
While I dance and skip, with a little wag.
But oh dear plant, you've got some bite,
Your prickles are fierce, but I still take flight.

"Look at my treasure!" I shout with glee,
While crickets laugh, just mocking me.
With growing pangs in this tongue-twisted spree,
Nature's joy is my remedy!

So I turn and twist, to see the light,
For in this green gold, I've found my delight.
Each petal and thorn tells a joke or two,
And here in the garden, I've reinvigorated the view!

Reflections Among the Thorns

In a garden of laughter, we trip and slip,
Brushing past blooms with a cheeky quip.
Each thorn a reminder of silly mistakes,
Yet in the jest, a sweet joy wakes.

We dance with the daisies, who giggle below,
While poking our fingers, oh, what a show!
With every sharp poke, there's laughter we share,
In this whimsical dance, we float in the air.

So here's to the moments of silly delight,
When prickles bring giggles, oh what a sight!
Amidst all the thorns, we'll never lose track,
For laughter is the prize that we'll never lack.

The Language of the Prickly

Speaking in prickles, the flowers all laugh,
They squawk out their secrets like a crazy giraffe.
A bouquet of humor in shades of bright green,
Where giggles and jabs make the silliest scene.

With a wink and a poke, they share all their tales,
Through wriggles and jibes, like wind in their sails.
Each prick is a tickle, each stem holds a joke,
In the language of flowers, laughter awoke.

Oh, listen closely to their giggly lore,
Behind every sharp point, there's a punchline galore.
So next time you wander, take heed of each sound,
For in the heart of gardens, true fun can be found.

Tenacious Dreams

In gardens where dreams stubbornly sprout,
Every tiny thorn knows what life's about.
Sticking to positivity like thorns on a rose,
With a grin and a poke, the laughter just flows.

We chase after wishes with our heads in the skies,
Tumbling through tangles and twinkling goodbyes.
Each little sharp challenge just fuels our drive,
In this crazy patch, we joyfully thrive.

So long as there's laughter amidst all the pricks,
Every tumble and trip feels just like a fix.
In the wild jungle of dreams, we twirl and we play,
For laughter, dear friend, is the light of our day.

Portrait of the Thorn

A portrait of prickles in shades of bright fun,
They twirl and they twist, like a dance in the sun.
Each thorn like a brushstroke on laughter's grand frame,
With humor in chaos, they play a wild game.

The world sees their sharpness, but we see the wit,
In the heart of each thorn, true mischief is lit.
With a flick and a twist, they tell stories of glee,
Through a wrap of green laughter, they beckon us free.

So here's to the thorns, the jesters of green,
In every sharp edge, a jovial scene.
For life's just a canvas, and joy paints it bright,
In the garden of giggles, we dance through the night.

Shadows Among the Brambles

In a garden where shadows play,
The brambles hold secrets, come what may.
A squirrel darts, a bird takes flight,
Curly tendrils snagging at night.

Laughter echoes from afar,
As critters ponder, 'Is that a car?'
The dandelions giggle with glee,
While the thorns just tease, 'Don't mess with me!'

A Thorny Medley of Dreams

A hedgehog winks, it's quite the scene,
With thorny fences, red and green.
The daisies dance, oh what a sight,
As bees all buzz to the left and right.

Each petal whispers a comedic tune,
While moonlit antics make flowers swoon.
A lazy cat watches from a chair,
Thinking, 'Did I leave my lunch out there?'

Stubborn Petals in the Breeze

Petals swaying, refusing to fall,
Holding on tightly to their tall wall.
In a gust, they tumble for fun,
Chasing shadows until they're done.

A ladybug laughs as it rides the wave,
While ants, in awe, work hard and brave.
With giggles exploding from flower to flower,
The garden's alive, it's time to devour!

Reflections in a Spiky Mirror

In puddles, the brambles have a chuckle,
As reflections dance in a wild huddle.
A mischievous rabbit hops with flair,
"What's with the spikes? I just need some air!"

Beneath the sun, they all behave,
Making jest of the way they wave.
A prickly crew, but never mean,
Their jests like bubbles, light and clean!

Between the Petal and the Thorn

In a garden where giggles pop,
Petals dance like they just can't stop.
Thorns are grumpy, with tough old frowns,
While blossoms twirl in pastel gowns.

Bees buzz loudly, with chubby cheer,
Trying to catch a whiff of beer.
With every sip, they drop and roll,
Do flowers laugh, or play the fool?

A snail in shades slips down a stem,
Waving to bugs, a real tough gem.
He tells grand tales of leafy lore,
While wishing for a dance on the floor.

The sun gets jealous of flower show,
And slips on shades, trying to glow.
In this patch of laughter so bright,
Thorns, you're not winning this comedic fight.

Grit Among the Petals

In the meadow, where petals sway,
Gritty tales of the clumsy play.
A bumblebee lost his way to lunch,
And bumped a rose in a hurried crunch.

Dandelions, with a cheeky grin,
Throw seeds around, let the chaos begin.
Rabbits hop in line, doing a jig,
While worms just wiggle, feeling rather big.

The gardener trips, spilling his seeds,
Sending angry ants on weird misdeeds.
"Oh no!" he shouts, "You pesky pests!
Do this again, and I'll take no requests!"

But flowers giggle, and leaf it be,
Nature's a stage, can't you see?
With grit among petals, life's set to laugh,
As each silly moment becomes a photograph.

The Heart of the Wild

In the heart where the wild things play,
Grasshoppers jam in a funky ballet.
A fox named Fred tries to catch a tune,
While moonslight strut beneath a silly moon.

With twirling leaves and whimsical breeze,
The trees gossip with the buzzing bees.
"Did you hear how the otter slipped?
He tried to dance but took a dip!"

A raccoon sings with tone-deaf glee,
While squirrels argue about the best tree.
In this joyful sprawl, no cares in sight,
The wild beats on, under starlit night.

So leave your worries at the open gate,
Join the jamboree, it's never too late.
With the heart of the wild, all jesters unite,
In laughter and mischief, life's pure delight.

Spines of Forgotten Ideas

Amidst the spines so stoic and grand,
Lie whispers of dreams, both clumsy and planned.
A squirrel named Simon sat down to think,
"Which nut's the best? I'll listen, not blink!"

Around him, thoughts bounce like a bouncy ball,
Saying ideas which might seem small.
But one lost seed told of a grand feast,
Of wild nut parties, a colorful beast!

The shadows chuckled, the sun gave a wink,
As the garden bubbled, making you think.
Those spines of ideas, once buried in grime,
Now dance on the edges, like poetry in rhyme.

So gather your musings, and let them be free,
For laughter's the prize, can't you see?
In the garden's embrace, the fun never ends,
With spines of forgotten ideas as friends.

The Resilience of Nature's Quills

In the garden, pricks and pokes,
Nature wears her spiky cloaks.
With a grin, she holds her ground,
In her fortress, joy is found.

Bouncing back with every poke,
She chuckles at the silly bloke.
Who dares to sneak and take a glance,
At her wild and spunky dance.

The bees buzz while they play tag,
In her arms, they never lag.
Even storms and droughts conspire,
To fuel her fun, ignite her fire.

Unruly friend with quills so bold,
Her antics never leave us cold.
In this jest of life, she sings,
A tale of joy and endless springs.

Unearthed Echoes of Quiet Defiance

From cracks in pavement, laughter bursts,
Waves of whimsy, jokingly cursed.
Roots defy, stretching low and wide,
Spreading giggles with great pride.

Whispers travel through the soil,
Making mischief, sharing toil.
Little spines that tickle, tease,
Lifting spirits with such ease.

Sun-kissed days bring cheeky fun,
While shadows spark the daring run.
Hey there, come and join the race,
In this wild and silly place.

Each sprout a rebel, with a wink,
A toast to nature's jester's brink.
In every plot, there lies a jest,
An echo of the earth's own quest.

Barbed Musings at Dawn

Morning breaks with chuckles bright,
Nature preens in soft sunlight.
Spines glisten in the golden glow,
Sharing secrets that they know.

A sip of dew, the day begins,
As laughter dances, nature grins.
Should you touch, you'd feel the prick,
But oh, the joy! A clever trick.

Birds cackle tunes among the thorns,
While bumblebees wear floral adorns.
With every flutter, they declare,
A world of whimsy everywhere.

In this tapestry of green,
Life unfolds, a playful scene.
Come marvel at the cheerful show,
Amidst the spikes, the good vibes flow.

The Beauty of Impenetrable Silence

In the stillness, laughter brews,
Among the thicket, cheer ensues.
Nature giggles in muted tones,
Where silence masks her playful bones.

A quiet dance beneath the trees,
Where gentle whispers tease the breeze.
The prickly ones hold court so sly,
With cheeky grins, they catch the eye.

Even without a noisy shout,
The world spins round with joy, no doubt.
For in the hushed, sublime embrace,
Nature spins her funny grace.

So wander through this peaceful place,
Where quiet sparkles with a trace.
Among the barbs, a jest exists,
A silent wink that can't be missed.

Twisted Reflections

In a mirror, a cactus grins,
Prickly jokes, where laughter begins.
With a wink, it tells a pun,
Under the sun, it's the only one.

Giggling blooms, in riotous cheer,
Spiting bees, they swat with great fear.
Dancing weeds twirl with flair,
Silly shadows, twirling without a care.

Tickled petals, in a wild spree,
Chasing squirrels up a tree.
In this patch, all wits run loose,
What a riot! Let laughter produce.

Spiky laughter in the air,
Each one sporting a funny hair.
Nature's jester, come take a look,
In the garden, fun's the only book.

In the Garden of Shadows

Whispers chuckle in the gloom,
Under petals, secrets loom.
Gnarled roots with little tricks,
Playing games like crafty chicks.

A shadow sprout, wearing a hat,
Calls its friends, and they all chat.
With a jive, they start to sway,
Making music in a leafy ballet.

Hopping sprites, in laughter drip,
At unseen gnomes who take a trip.
Fairy tales in clumsy flights,
Twirling tales in soft moonlight.

In dim corners, where sun hides,
You will find where the fun abides.
These frolics, under watchful eyes,
Make even gloom wear a silly guise.

Barbed Elegy

A thorny joke hangs in the air,
With laughter caught, it strips bare.
In vines of humor, tangled tight,
Prickly yet funny, they take flight.

A hedgehog tripped on a fool's stroll,
Pulled a prank, and stole the whole.
Flowers chuckled, they knew well,
Barbed humor casts a funny spell.

With every sting, a riot blooms,
A prick here and there, amidst the boom.
Injuries shared become a laugh,
Finding joy in each thorny path.

From these spines, wit does arise,
Cackling blooms beneath the skies.
Nature's lesson, quick to share,
Find the fun in every snare.

Vexed Petals

Petals puff, in comic plight,
Swatting bugs in a silly fight.
With flustered grace, they shake and spin,
As nature's giggles start to win.

A rose went mad, pricked its own nose,
Dancing around in elaborate clothes.
Bumblebees laugh, with buzzing glee,
At this fashion—in a floral spree.

Under the sun, they plot and scheme,
Every bloom shares a secret dream.
Witty verses whirl about,
In this garden, there's no doubt.

Vexed petals, yet full of cheer,
Tickling the breeze that draws near.
Join the jaunt in petal's embrace,
Where every snag finds a funny place.

The Nettle's Song

In a garden wild and free,
A netty song we sing with glee.
Prickles dance in the morning sun,
A laugh, a jab, oh what fun!

Bumblebees buzz, feeling bold,
Tickling toes, or so I'm told.
They sip the nectar, not a care,
While we prickle, but they're unaware.

Winds whisper secrets, we jive along,
Each sharp edge adds to the song.
With every bump and tiny sting,
Life's a laugh when nettles sing!

So if you wander through this patch,
Watch your step, or you'll catch a scratch.
But join the dance, don't be afraid,
In our spiky world, memories are made!

Dances with Spines

In the thicket where the prickles play,
I wiggle my toes, come what may.
A spiky partner, oh so spry,
We twirl beneath the cloudy sky.

With every shuffle, a laugh erupts,
I stumble and trip, oh life disrupts!
Yet those sharp hugs bring silly cheer,
A prickly dance, I hold you near.

Around and around, we spin and sway,
Through tangles and knots, we find our way.
Embracing the bumps, we leap and glide,
In this crazy waltz, we take great pride!

So grab a spine, don't be quite shy,
Let's dance in thorns and laugh up high.
For in this laughter, sharp as a knife,
We find the joy that brightens life!

Hidden Resilience

Beneath the surface, oh what a sight,
A stubborn heart twinkles bright.
Furry leaves hide tales of old,
In every rustle, wisdom told.

Through tangled paths, we push on through,
With laughter and grit, the world feels new.
We may be prickled, but still we stand,
Making sunshine in barren land.

A little giggle from each sharp point,
Shows resilience when we disappoint.
For every sting brings forth a chance,
To find that strength in life's own dance.

So raise a toast to all the thorns,
In every heart where laughter's born.
For underneath, we're full of cheer,
Embracing life without a fear!

Musing with the Briars

Through briar bushes, I wander wide,
With tangled thoughts that seem to hide.
Each thorny twist a laugh it brings,
As nature plays, and joy takes wing.

I muse aloud, just me and spines,
In leafy company, no need for signs.
Entangled dreams and giggles neat,
In the wild garden, life's a treat!

While climbing high, my feet get stuck,
Oh dear, a tangle! What a cluck!
But in this mess, I find delight,
Briars can make the heart feel light.

So let's embrace the prickle's charm,
Nature's humor, a warming balm.
With laughter echoing through the trees,
Together we muse, with playful ease!

Serendipity Amongst the Spikes

In a garden full of pricks, so spry,
A chipmunk danced, oh my, oh my!
With every leap, he felt the sting,
But laughter echoed; joy's the thing.

A little bee, with buzz so bold,
Complained of woes, a tale retold.
"These spikes, I swear, have got my name!"
Yet still, he stuck around the game.

The flowers laughed, their petals bright,
At furry friends in silly flight.
A comedy of nature's play,
Mixed joy and pricks in bright array.

So sway, dear friends, through prickly paths,
With laughter shared, forget your wraths.
For in the thorns, the fun convenes,
And prickle tales sprout joyful scenes.

Beneath a Cactus Sky.

Beneath a sky with cacti tall,
A tortoise tripped, and then did sprawl.
With spiky friends around his shell,
He pondered life—then laughed as well.

A lizard slid with snickers sly,
"Don't worry friend, just give a try!"
"These points are sharp, but fear not fate,"
"Embrace the fun; it's never late!"

The flowers giggled in the breeze,
As shadows danced among the trees.
A playful poke, a gentle tease,
Nature's jesters, aiming to please.

With every poke, a tale to weave,
The joy of life, so hard to leave.
So stroll beneath this prickly spire,
Where joy and laughter never tire.

Prickled Whispers

In a patch where whispers play,
A hedgehog rolled, come what may.
"Oh dear, am I poking fun?"
Laughter echoed, heels were run.

A wise old owl with a funny quirk,
Sat grinning wide, smirking with perk.
"In sharpest company, joy is found,"
"So come, my friends, let's twirl around!"

In every thorn, a tale resides,
Of silly slips and playful slides.
"One must be brave to laugh so loud,"
Said the busy bee—proud and crowd!

So gather near, you quirky bunch,
In blades of green, we'll munch and crunch.
For life's a jest, let humor glide,
Among the spikes, our joy won't hide.

A Bloom of Dilemmas

In the garden of curious blooms,
A snail pondered all his dooms.
"Shall I cheat fate and speed on by?"
"Or linger long and wave goodbye?"

A flower grinned with petals wide,
"Just take your time; it's quite the ride!"
"With every doubt, let giggles sprout,"
"For life's a riddle, without a doubt!"

A bumblebee stumbled on a thorn,
"Oh my, who knew that I was born?"
"To hug the plants with such a flair,"
"To slip and trip without a care!"

So dance amidst these prickly fates,
And join the choir that celebrates.
For in every dilemma, a laugh we find,
In the blooms of life, we're intertwined.

The Song of the Uninvited Flora

In a garden where no one prunes,
A twist of fate sings silly tunes.
With roots that giggle in the ground,
They dance to rhythms quite profound.

Poking fun at all that's neat,
They throw a party on the street.
With leaves adorned in playful pride,
Odd little blooms, no place to hide.

They jest with bees that buzz in glee,
And share their laughs with every bee.
A patch of chaos, full of cheer,
In this wild spot, they persevere.

So raise a glass to wayside cheer,
To those bold blooms we all hold dear.
Uninvited but so sublime,
Bringing joy in every rhyme.

Resilience Wrapped in Spike

Amidst the bramble, sharp and spry,
A quirk of nature makes us sigh.
With prickly charms and sneaky flair,
They smile and giggle, unaware.

In gardens where the posies pout,
These brave ones laugh and twist about.
They poke their heads so proud and tall,
A spiky jest for one and all.

When daisies flaunt their silken grace,
The spiky folks don't lose their place.
With stubborn roots and a hearty grin,
They know the fun is born within.

So let us cheer for those who stick,
Beneath the sun, they're truly slick.
Wrapped in charm, with toughness too,
These thorns are laughter breaking through.

Whimsies Amidst the Brash

In fields of folly, flowers play,
They jostle 'round, come what may.
With colors clashing, oh so bright,
They throw a bash that feels just right.

The daisies roll their eyes so wide,
At foliage that won't abide.
They dance in tunes no one can hear,
With nature's whimsies spreading cheer.

The rude weeds join, with cheeky grins,
In a madcap tale where fun begins.
Each petal smiles, a witty jest,
In a world where laughter is the best.

So let the brash take center stage,
For every bloom, a different page.
Together they bloom, a colorful clash,
With buoyant hearts in a daring dash.

Petals Against the Grit

In the cracks where no one looks,
Sweet petals peek, like open books.
Defying odds, they wink and sway,
In laughter's grip, they find their way.

With grit beneath, they firmly stand,
As life throws challenges unplanned.
With every wind that seeks to blame,
They giggle back, "What's in a name?"

They dance through rain, with colors bright,
Persuading storm clouds to take flight.
So let the hard times come and go,
These blooms know well how to steal the show.

In every crack, they claim their spot,
With petals bold and laughter hot.
Against the grit, they sow delight,
And turn the dark to sheer delight.

Whispers of the Wildflower

In a patch of grass they sway,
The daisies chat all day.
"Look at us, so bright and bold,
While the weeds feel tired and old!"

Bumblebees join in the jest,
Buzzing loud, they never rest.
"Why be neat, when chaos sings?
Life's a dance, let's spread our wings!"

Buttercups giggle in applause,
As dandelions boast their flaws.
"We're the kings of the sunlit glen,
A little mud never hurt our zen!"

So let's frolic in the breeze,
Forget our worries, just be at ease.
For in this wildflower's fun-filled grove,
Even the prickliest begin to rove!

Prickled Reverie

A cactus thought it quite a thrill,
To wear a crown of spiky frills.
"Look at me, I'm so unique,
A walking poke that loves to speak!"

The roses mocked, all soft and sweet,
"Your sharpness can't compete with our heat!"
They giggled as they swayed in grace,
While the prickly one turned red in face.

But in this garden filled with cheer,
Even thorns can find a peer.
"Let's toast to weirdness, here's a toast,
To those who shine and those we boast!"

Amid the laughter, petals flew,
Friendship blooms, both old and new.
For those who giggle, nudge, and tease,
Have hearts that blossom, always please!

The Thorned Mind's Garden

In the garden of tangled thoughts,
A daisy wrestles with what it's caught.
"Should I bloom or hide away?
Life's a riddle, come what may!"

A sunflower cracked a joke,
"Don't take life too serious, or it'll choke!"
With petals wide and seeds in hand,
They made plans for a bloom-filled band.

The violets cheered, all inked with glee,
"Let's celebrate our quirky spree!
With each mishap, let laughter ring,
We'll dance as if we're on a swing!"

No shame in thorns, they took the stage,
While laughter danced upon every page.
In this wild garden, thoughts intertwine,
Making fizzles and giggles, oh so divine!

Echoes of the Unruly Bloom

Our garden's an uproar of cheer,
Where petals bounce and wiggly deer.
"Why behave when you can shout?
In wild blooms, there's no doubt!"

A rogue flower raised its voice,
"In my chaos, I rejoice!
Let mischief sprout like every weed,
For in laughter, we're all freed!"

Hummingbirds in fits of glee,
Dizzy from the nectar spree.
They zipped and zoomed, what a sight!
Making flowers giggle in delight.

So let us toast to every petal deep,
And giggle when the garden creaks.
For in the ruckus of color's bloom,
Lies the joy that chases gloom!

Metaphors from the Brambles

In a garden where the brambles grow,
The jokes are sharp, and the giggles flow.
Each thorny laugh hides a silly twist,
Poking fun at the hairdresser's mist.

When bees wear hats and dance on a whim,
The daisies will chuckle; they're never grim.
A wild vine tickles the nose of a frog,
While shadows play tag with the sun, like a dog.

Twisted vines share stories, oh so grand,
Of frogs in tuxedos who can't understand.
Laughter erupts from the roots underground,
As mushrooms perform in a whimsical round.

In bramble thickets, the mirthful reside,
With giggling bunnies, they share joy with pride.
Amidst the chaos, they poke fun with glee,
Who knew that humor could grow from a tree?

The Riddle of the Root

Beneath the soil, where secrets lie,
Roots share riddles as they bounce and pry.
What's green and yellow and dances all night?
A confused carrot who took a wrong flight!

The acorns gossip, throwing shade like a pro,
"Did you hear the one about the veggie who'd grow?
He thought he was tall, but sadly he found,
He was just a cucumber, thought lost and confound."

Then gathered the snails for a quick comedy act,
With shells as their props, they never lacked tact.
A slug slipped on stage with a slippery grin,
"Why didn't the lettuce want to be thin?"

The roots kept chuckling at the playful jest,
Even the earthworms couldn't help but rest.
For below, where the fun is a plucky pursuit,
Laughter grows deep—just like every root!

Blooming in Dissonance

In the flashy patch where the blooms don't agree,
A peony shouts, "Come dance with me!"
But the daisies roll eyes, all stiff and uptight,
Saying, "We'd rather just soak up the light."

A sunflower tries to win over the weeds,
"Join in my chorus, let's ignore the creeds!"
But the violets giggle, "Oh dear, we're shy,
Don't you see, oh sun, you're much too high!"

With colors conflicting, they sway with glee,
"Who needs a melody, let's just let it be!"
A bumblebee chuckles, leaving petals in dismay,
"Should I sing for you all? Or just fly away?"

Yet amidst the discord, a friendship bloomed,
Through jests and laughter, all jealousy roomed.
Each flower unique, a comical sight,
Who knew chaos could feel so right?

Whims of the Weeds

Oh the weeds have dreams that soar so high,
"Let's take to the skies and learn how to fly!"
They gather at dusk in a raucous parade,
While tulips just tremble, afraid of the shade.

A clover spreads tales of lands far and wide,
With stories of daisies who learned how to glide.
The thistles are plotting a game of charades,
"Who's the best dancer?" they debate in cascades.

Hedgerow whispers float through the air,
As dandelions propose, "Why not go bare?"
A prickle, a poke, leaves them all in delight,
While grasses all chuckle, with roots gripping tight.

For in their wild whims, they find merriment,
In every rough patch lies a laughter's intent.
So let's raise a toast to the weeds and their cheer,
For in their own chaos, there's nothing to fear!

In the Heart of Prickles

In a garden of greens and spines,
I laughed at the weeds in their lines.
They poke and they prod, oh what a sight,
Dancing around in the warm sunlight.

A bumblebee buzzed with a frown,
"Why wear these thorns? It brings you down!"
I giggled and shrugged as I twisted my hair,
"Life's a party, just beware of the flare!"

With petals so flashy, each one a tease,
We join in the chaos, swaying with ease.
Who knew that prickles could spark such delight?
Every poke tells a story, oh what a sight!

So here's to the humor, the jests that abound,
In a world full of spines, there's joy all around.
Let laughter ring out where the oddities grow,
In the heart of the prickly, let's steal the show!

Reflections in a Verdant World

Amidst the green foliage, dancing with glee,
A cactus is posing, so fancy and free.
"Look at me glimmer, with spikes as my bling!"
I chuckle and ponder, what else can he bring?

In puddles of sunshine, a snail takes her time,
Each inch is a journey, a climb without rhyme.
"Why rush?" she exclaims with a wink and a grin,
"It's not about speed; it's the fun that we're in!"

There's humor in curling leaves, acting like jesters,
The flowers throw tantrums; they're ultimate testers.
They pout and they puff, when the breezes play rough,
But a tickle from rain shows they're strong, sure enough!

In this verdant world, let silliness bloom,
With roots that connect us like threads in a loom.
Let laughter ripen where quirkiness sways,
In reflections of nature, we'll brighten our days!

Blossoms of Struggle

In a field of oddities, blooms burst with flair,
Each petal is laughing, without a single care.
"We bloom where we're planted, despite all our woes!"
Whispers the dandelion, wearing his clothes.

The roses are sulking, all wrapped up in pride,
While the clovers are giggling, they cannot abide.
"You think you're so grand with your fragrance and hue,"

But there's charm in our mess, just look at our view!"

Poking through cracks, weeds plot their escapades,
In a game of hide-and-seek, they parade.
"Catch me if you can!" says the mischievous sprout,
As the daisies roll laughter, there's no room for doubt.

So here's to the battles that nature bestows,
In the blossoms of struggle, true character grows.
With each prick and poke, we take life with cheer,
For in playful resilience, we conquer all fear!

Prickly Contemplation

In the silence of shade, where the oddities dwell,
A hedgehog is pondering; he has stories to tell.
"Why do I wear armor? What's wrong with my style?"
He ponders and chuckles, taking a while.

The porcupine joins with a nod and a grin,
"It's hard to be friendly when you're covered in chin!"
Yet they laugh at the thought of their prickly embrace,
Finding fun in their features, a curious space.

Beneath shifting shadows, they play hide and seek,
Sharing secrets of nature with laughter unique.
"We're not just sharp things! We're soft in our hearts,
Behind all these quills, there are wonderful parts!"

In prickly contemplation, they bask in the light,
Finding solace in friendship, in the day and the night.
So when life gets too poky, don't shudder or pout,
Just twirl with your spines, and dance it all out!

The Beauty of the Barbed

In a garden so bright, with colors so bold,
A prickly surprise shyly unfolds.
With a wink and a nod, it stands with a grin,
It's the spiky delight that dares you to spin.

Bumblebees buzzing, in laughter they flit,
While I trip over roots, and they find it a hit.
Poke me, I'll whisper, it's all in good fun,
For the barbed little jester shines brighter than sun.

In a patch of delight, it steals all the show,
With laughter so loud, that the daisies won't grow.
Each stem a mischief, each bloom a sly jest,
This thorny comedian is simply the best.

Fractured Yet Flourishing

In a world made of giggles, where humor's a seed,
A fractured old plant blooms with magnificent speed.
With a wink as it bends, and a chuckle it sways,
While dodging the raindrops, it dances for days.

The more that it bends, the more laughter it brings,
With every sharp edge, it also can sing.
Who knew the odd shape could brighten the day?
A rebel of nature, hip-hip-hooray!

Amidst chuckles and snorts, it flaunts its delight,
For the quirks of the world make it bloom even bright.
A comedy show in a garden's grand court,
With nature as jesters, laughter's the sport.

Thorns Beneath the Surface

With a smile 'neath layers of prickly disguise,
A cheeky little plant spins tales of surprise.
Don't be fooled by the cover, it's ready to play,
Poking at life in the silliest way.

Underneath those sharp edges, there's always a twinkle,
Catch the whimsy, the fun, in its delightful sprinkle.
It chuckles and giggles when you're not around,
Making mischief and magic without making a sound.

Like a riddle in bloom, it teases your heart,
Embracing the chaos, it plays its own part.
Yet in shadows it's grinning, the joy it will craft,
For the thorns hold the laughter that's always unmasked.

An Untamed Reverie

In a field of the wild where the oddbirds all roam,
This scrappy old flower calls chaos its home.
With petals askew, and a laugh so sincere,
It spins wild daydreams and chases a cheer.

Cactus in dance shoes, all clumsy and proud,
Wobbling about, making mischief so loud.
With a jig and a jab, it leads the parade,
An untamed performer, an oddball - unafraid!

Each poke tells a story, each petal a song,
In a world full of normal, it happily throngs.
So here's to the wild, the weird, and the free,
Where laughter erupts, and the oddities flee.